SPLIT THE STICK:
A MINIATURIST-DIVAN

SPLIT THE STICK:
A MINIATURIST-DIVAN

Mac Wellman

ROOF BOOKS
NEW YORK

ISBN: 978-1-931824-46-0
Library of Congress Catalog Card Number: 2012931681

Cover: Majnun Approaches the Camp of Layla's Caravan,
from Haft Awrange by Jami,1556-65

Acknowledgements
Some of these poems have appeared in: *The Boston Review, Heights
of the Marvelous* and Sun & Moon Press's *Gertrude Stein Poetry Awards,
Critical Quarterly* and *Words Worth*. In addtion, the third section *The
Rat Minaret,* is published in the LRL Textile series.

Thanks to the Rockefeller Study and Conference Center in Bellagio, Italy.

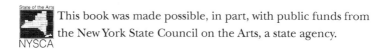 This book was made possible, in part, with public funds from
the New York State Council on the Arts, a state agency.

Roof Books are distributed by
Small Press Distribution
1341 Seventh Street
Berkeley, CA. 94710-1403
Phone orders: 800-869-7553
www.spdbooks.org

Roof Books are published by
Segue Foundation
300 Bowery
New York, NY 10012
seguefoundation.com

Contents

SPRUNG

Contents

DOPE (AS IN IDIOT)

Pinko lives in a school of rabbit

toils

while a

bitchery of whiles,

each one of them

alone, indifferent

to the benthonic, what pushes.

Below.

Below boxed in a Pinko

Plot, a

❋

Boxes of peaches. No school

lords

booms! About the common pouch

sweets, O

pulchritude! What

another run at the presidency?

＊

Incriminates

skirmisher

rock bite. At

firing the

wholesale

A to B,

is played out.

＊

A door ajar as

sale

sorbid? Sorbid. Down

slide to dead places

where

stills of Manasses grind at the

cheek:

Quake slide down to an absolute any

＊

Causeless question to a

window flush

sad to

balk;

melange

crises

thoughts for sale. Can't

❋

Creative conditions the

Apex. Undue

Birdseed

feigns a disregard for

an asterisk's

the bone of trees. Swift

jawbone's

❋

Bakelite

Sandusky. Radios

who

darn

who

to

quilts. Am I

?

✤

Sierra.

Tops

is

towing the

grinning...

As in.

Porch of those who collect the old

✤

As in "dumb";

cause a fright

hair.

No cash down —

decode deco.

Rumble

witness a cream

up

stand up and be

❋

Ray

's

goons

a cycle of dare. Quite

mens

too;

❋

Tubal

Baksheesh

callow

x'd

boomerangs. A

con

victorious!

as board can

woo'd. Watch out for

W

An

dam. A water hitched to a

remote

of pitching other weird woo;

MELOYD GREATOVER

Perform cat before the moon was

a greatwilly up.

Twill...

wows,

A all the way to B and

askew

just think about it;

❋

Just an unemployed landapaperwawafofod

who

too, it

a crazy licence to

pronk...

barroom —

Woozy nesting place, a

swaying un

owned. Beings

*

one sleek dotted i

kayo'd

You the Pindar

imaginary:

Rudolf Valentino

Rudolf the red-nosed reindeer

Rudolf Hitler...

All Rudolfs to the nth

*

I find obsequious is

in was

and therefore whet

Occam's

a class of consternation up-ended

A to B, hey, that's

mnemonic

a hummer

where

to do it

best...

＊

The silence wishes

who best

darken door

door

the

back to A and no cigar.

Grasshopper without a

Convair. Mecca.

＊

Best to best and who's the

tragic blond

once upon a

Bed.

Red the greatwilly

O

and all O unboxed:

17

shoe me, baby

✻

Quartz the peppercorn

observe all meloyd greatwillies

till.

X the schemer

unkinds the yarn

O fate fraught, O

cairn!

rollover and sky

back to A. The end.

✻

Not kiss no apple mouse's

tips

yet toes

heel to clarity. Over the hell

bore

heart's Y.

in clover. Rollover and

jumpy like...

✼

A waxen

whatchamacallit

a various slowdown

mummy

sandstone

kill the bone dark, kill the

death stone.

Cellod. An old word for nythery....

Split the stick,

✼

Find out who

chucked what

bazaar

checked what

a whimsy of curlicues

Fun the un

American:

I invent alloys and am allowed to.

I am a landapaperwawafofod

All kind of him are.

Over the best, the worst as B

back to A

the best, the best

❀

Solemn

cat face;

a hick once. Now a

highness sorts

Greatover...

Solar bean to B

whiskey

❀

No coat but wholly mine

do the dare

no mimic music.

no bent whistle

Power's

best broiling rainbow

stay the

Glacier...

corn rules and we

comic

8 ball

too dome

a

kinda meloyd

pluck it

❋

Point out

jubilation city

thumpa

pail a

bucket water in hand

W

Some great galoot

Storm

She the Who

S' CAN

...future is all behind me now, my

it

hopes;

glider with a

black-eyed Susan...

serendipitous;

❋

Show me a thing

pell mell

corked on

haywire...

Explain the

bug

to

❋

Upside down

no pout

looking for a

can.

Quandary

no music in this

one, two

＊

Red Angel

on coasters

Quite.

A regular pile-on

of illness. Too

puppy

＊

Live it up till the

whole in the air sink

Y (Y?)

cozy in the dram...

You, and

who's to pay

up, down, a sequence

❉

Wish I would go

no

hell is here and there;

So

a cold city without no postcards

away, away!

❉

Sad to fair the

dark one, a

fornication flies up, needle in a mad brightness

to be gotten dreamer

at. Pay no mind.

❉

My sister, my seem-

O!

fine tone.

Chaos hardly what a gal likes

I am.

Pushover peckerwood.

❉

Tiny the tune as a fruitcake walk-on

fine out. What's

so if the

bust is all wonderment?

Ask a question.

The....

❉

Scarcely had it be

dimmed

to be dumb! I

older

Miscreant. Monster. Mover & Shaker

Always, light the intellect, doing it my way

Un-

Whipped. For the blood play's done.

A

*

Split the stick & find

*

Questionmark.

slid;

a supple

neck and

72 sweaters heaped up in

wood.

place your hand, all of it, in mine

*

This notorious zig-zag of mine

overlook and

balustrade. Super

thin

Wiggles and X

irt

votes too, and will.

*

Quite the

pains me till up

spikes

the cookie jar. Ape

Not the style of acting, not the

theatre you

shoes;

Get it?

A IS APEST, B IS BIGGEST BANANA REPUBLIC

Yawn the real American

Callithumpian hayride.

fract

dope

(as in...)

lulu

its;

*

poison

a belated

to stillness

Quack.

Done.

Bark up the

*

Castle in the

aeroplane.

Seek. A passing

beauty. Should I

tempt the

fractal...

Mass the dark ones there,

Executive and

auto-

clemency. A rule of thumb

Quite the

Bottleneck. A to

do it

baksheesh. Day glide and

Day's

Air. The dollars'

Split the stick & find

the

one whose sorrow,

the one whose care

is a Small, the

Smallest

Sparkle of mica, shows

(w)here?

＊

Very.

Very, very much...

so

tilt the wizard of the

worm and

... front moved. Oldish word

Cellod , oldest not

Known, a knowing not

Creatured in inkst

gladdens.

Hope. I build my own house of cards.

with ancestors. Logic!

Park. In the

sky's

*

Act. Phone.

too

bliss a

rotate

the

warring was

wrecked and why not?

Super

combustible

I'm

*

The

in

Y

poorest of

?

...

Cello

is mumps.

Where;

Phony. No gadget

shows

Owning up.

A

tuneful melody at

realignment's

hobo...

"bos"

❈

Some there are already.

They talk

X

is sprung. To be

not to be

the cops hate

it disremembers how

gangland bought

shoes in and out

broke; and the close-out

tin

(as in...)

＊

homeless, wet and cold

fan doors

till...

eye on the numbers

cloud climbs red,

waste!

Strike the stick and hear its

Crie:

I

out

here, there

＊

and Spring is what

o

how to

post a quick message to

all who

and bed the

toes.

My gripes'

on tenterhooks...

Nope,

A SWINDLE OF WINDOWS

Fluorescence. I

stand up and be counted

Till

a gander

Got.

Cuomo bumps

(Means of power nixed

Exercise thereof

To this very day. Darn doubled)

✢

Bleakest

Topaz. O

was

wasn't.

as is

the stage whisper

sinkest.

＊

Blue;

attributes a

bottle to

camphor

Dance as dunce.

Elegaic

am footwear. O!

＊

Tipple music in plucked wave

Time's "foo".

the dart

Fashions a collide

dormer in.

Plunked down in Crows'

X.

＊

But the catch of the lock had not caught.

back weeds

what

to

too.

Insufficient types and

!

Wrongdoing. A
&

Knelt to

pocket of jet

position. Four

Square.

Up

to now,

&

Kissed.

Sanity

barb

pot

is

is.

Concentrate;

*

Bellowing

dinner

quirts

at bursting open to find

down —

3/8's...

ah

*

Ink most a trade mill to

more and

tin

bannister veering. Complete the

To the

Vote avoiding, un-

fed...

O rider, simply

one cuff in, one cuff out, cowboys

tanta

mount, psych

a

astonish

✻

a rotate of stiffener, no,

gurgle on

Pie.

No

Nope.

No frame for the turning, no here's

✻

Pips

to quite the kite...

Super industrial for X the rotate

glide to choice.

Can

Woodens

An?

*

An undertow of the disaffected, an

A inner

infinity of hat band and

hair oil:

Impossible imbricate

Of our own time

's told

to Who by Who, who

splits the stick to

touch a wall

Street grown wise with

No

School as a snow of her heaved papers.

Bomb

ball stone to give

Time. Time to inch up the

pseudo;

chill the wheel.

✻

Goldwater's

ice and carrot bought.

Box

ing

at a

Something the matter with all who

Un

THE LAST FULL MOON ON
FRIDAY THE THIRTEENTH
IN THE TWENTIETH CENTURY

As a book of sandpaper would.

loss and

hung.

Too

miracl'd

tests

agape

❋

hawks

hooped till

the bourne

pupped

a tizzy till

counter

dismals

a tuft at

radius with

OO

cats'

blade

✲

Out there

the precise

calligraphy, a

outlaw, a

staycool

ends.

Pointless to tell

✲

Whoever receives the cheese

I shall god

The Sky! The Sky!

itself out

an
Ever Wonder

Pix,

＊

Touches

at

to

gets goes

York

Heart's

The Knot

＊

O, assistant

noise maker,

Fair

the

wrestled with a stepladder;

wingtoo

wasn't.

＊

Too the knot to

nix.

Drave

at which can

wicca

(Cellod's little sister,

wicked grin, & shiny black

A tooth)

A slain

drumlin goes

✳

Face ban

Perhelion

potted. A

chair

ribbed. Over

cane break. O

That.

✳

Movie blued the

the

feign

holds out.

No coin, but

Spatters.

Gollywog's

gut

to, the

*

Dioptric

Bad luck's big hat saint day

nub

to

a

the manual of turns, up

nosed,

fancy's

O,
*

Archeozoic.

Archeopteryx.

Scratch the

till then. It's

a pardon kept

pillows.

what golds up and glister

＊

Go and

Bed.

Cross the moon-silver

until a

momentous...

Death figures to

inner room

Beat, beat.

NEUF-NEUF

A flurry of hands, hands

Can.

to a dis-

Rider out. Put in and

O

the way reaches to.

This, that

Rider, how

how

Bald wand of shoes, gloves, hats, all

*

Sprays the

temperature

bollide. For

bulldog Wuffles

knows Iraq's Winston's

mooring-screw — alas

for the rest of us

Hashemites, Cuomo,

Rider's split stick and all.

Dislikes also

split the stick.

Fix a

Rider that
is

a

at. Once at sunset on

moon,

✵

Silver rider and 7

a

past tense of a

painting. Fine wood. Rich

cases of vases. Clear

A riderless

60's

My

how

Despite the abdication. I don't accept

✳

Two numbers, the same

reaching for the cupboard

Jets

a

Rider just a

waste of my

Apple.

✳

A witnessing

don't I?

Anybody like who

so

soon the

bribery an accepted practice

moon on hair is,

rider

✼

Straight up, rider

stall

Bingo

and glide. A wing

snow falling in slow tufts till

motion. Abstract. Fact

fuzzy, too,

✼

Gentle rider

Ebon. O

isn't

✼

Too. The rider

upside down

Where?

Garland

More than any single can possibly

Bottle.

Surging

❀

A republic shoes it

boo...

whipsnake and black

bones. A

drilled

Awaken. Who

Rider was

Was

❀

Bank on considerable baloney

You who

American. Osterizer

picture

bum. Zoo

Try

sack and

Rider. 8 ball

*

Holy the

bricabrac —

Bashes.

it with

white too...

Bricabrac;

Baksheesh.

Our wars

whizz

Rider too;

ISMS & PRISMS:

(Seventh Book of Satires)

OF ISMS AND PRISMS

Cat in a graveyard, chasing her tail.

Quite the turnstile

feline. A prehensile

Periscope.

If you look sideways

forklift, training the light to

bend.

An ism of prism, an

✻

!

up that greasy, up that

thing of desperate keepsake

Time, my

Saves. By all the

purple hepatica

where mist the mark

dog silly

ups that greasy pole; and how

top hat. A double reverse

Burnt

＊

Framed, they crie. For all eyes

guide the hand

See? A

＊

Grasps. Air full with strange cries

sense of civic disorder. The human face

no ism to act upon as a

Rules the

the nort. Misology

and be XXX'd upon

up that greasy pole, boys, up

tombstones. All the

to gather the windfall

of Mister Professional Brown-Nose.

butt, o,

bites the

*

Up that greasy pole, ladies and

nope

a fear glides over the lit candles, hits

the hanged man, dead, swinging in upon

together. Seven of us

getting old and are wowed

to be.

*

7 chairs ...

wrung neck, poor

food man.

*

who knows the silly from the

Sally? who knows the

Silly from the best?

Worth a high price. Because

what counts, causes. The

Light fills all place with colors and air

rant fools. I am

Others. We go

in grace, without knowing

what I do. Churches

filled with old music, faith

bores the bleak with a

dog and cat's eye view. A pop

Who's.

the big zero ...

❋

Who hopes:

dreams of nothing, I'm

most careful with old mahogany.

❋

Thee?

with all her flagrant leaves

in a lacquered state.

sky, too, so

that and that too

flints;

focus shifting to

the point. Do you know

wooden thinks

as the flower of faith has fade

built right in. We hope...

*

in boxes; nor do I dare to gather

Water ...

in aire's name, as the crowe hies.

*

poor Starry,

filled with my boys

glad to glimmer

no face fastened —

golden codex, moon of struck gold

bent like a bird;

the people who tooled up, too

✻

heart's larceny

screwed up. To be sure

a scary

✻

close of some radionuclide adrift in the

willow-wind ...

bidding for a box-lunch fate, o,

✻

empty the sky is, empty of us

concrete. The noble sense of how

to a

? sunset. The sun

had to race.

For Starry, too, is a

matchbox artificer. Who has an odd

even's the devil-thread. Who

crows'

wax ... This, too, marks the surety

Straight from the sharp, acute in-

verse of cats. A cycle of cats and souls, each

an ideal premise

in a sorites of istic, ismistic

who-knows? Who!

the strange from the narrow? The

*

Orphaned

Widows, all

odd matches...

*

Empty casting ... Who?

whole hill, leaves scattered

passage. Shadows rippling down

idea; but there is still the old

beckons with a brightnesse, with no

seek the first dry things of Spring,

crooked thing of thorn, a

✤

A cross between cupid. And the devil pours

leans to the flow;

and the watch-faces are:

✤

because the devil was small, still a child

of lightnesse; till the breath

of one who is not

weakens the stone. For the moon's a

tourist here, on a ferry to

dreaming place. Where the azaleas

conspire and wind-up the

✤

witch-hunts.

Formalities will occur at the

Only at the Eastern

Corridor and floor to floor with

sparkle & cool water. A

shrubbery ferrets hillside,

brought about by luck; and yet

＊

pauses

Night the artifact

toe to toe with cats, a

wonder the

Y's cake. Pour

The cat walks, wind in her face ...

A wicked,

?

＊

barn. Give up hoping ...

over and over, shoes

boring through the solidest. To ex-

＊

In the holiest of times, death

there, thinking

A

lucky toss of the hat

A chronic

May wine. A boot, a shoe.

❋

wearing thin sure

with holes. The humble press upon the

whole sick

❋

nanocurie on the tongue glows;

seconds pass, you

badly off, and where?

Mister Hare in the barley.

flare, fly, fall.

Like the true man's tryst

dust, buried sky-high in the

Tootle.

To chisel the word from runic-work

did, o,

❋

hill in sky snows, white

Illusion: ghost of Mad's

Wilds the ...

Cats ...

Go wild and

keep. Stay away from eld

embedded alpha-emitters,

pipes and picoliters,

don't breathe: hope

The hot star in the lung's

not: for hope

hops. Yes,

tint the glade on the stone heap's baldy.

*

Stairway too. Give up candles and

Starry glows in clothes, too

an oddball river

peppers.

bingo parlors roar for Mars on the tide

flow of rats and

*

Catclatter. Catfool. Catperson ...

with all her flagrant colors

an outlaw.

*

greased lightning and

leave faith at door: under stone

lizard a cat spies. Bite, cat, bite!

For — on the floor —

,all cats know:

the ending is more starry than the door.

The cat on a gravestone

slides roundy about a

dubious creed. Strike the stick and

You will find *Jesus*

among other slants:

Faith is of the earth, like silver grasses

Gentle doubt makes an ism of —

into a prism. Ocularia. It reads

you right, human. The whole iron hill

abduct the art: The end goes on longer than the

Start; that's why it's

called "the end"

The Rat Minaret

=

LOST from an ingevonic
isostasy. Lime
disc, South…
you and
SILVERY —

All sticks are equally struck.

~

O fanciest fan choral
vat brilliant violet,
here the flixweed's …

~

AIRY disc tipped up and on
silvery
an X and

~

A line of triple X's are earmarked, go
to screw the,
Pan-
dora,
go and catch a

takes it to
the only "ism";
Y the ceremony
Y the cereus;
Close the clack-valve, the

~

Odd's sake takes the risk.
An immolation
in
the name of whose day.

No match, or if one,
no gasoline;

who runs this joint? Not a who

known to Peekaboo.

~

As ever, both imperial and anticanonical,
Silvery's
mad
fools none, but
fuels the dark.

Dim departure's
black light.

~

Go to A one less could be a nightmarish
nickel
wallop,
X the

~

CLASSIC urn-wallow and hop to hope to
snip from agenbite,
mealybug, took
to Bazerlies Cylinders;
not bay-bay, no,
nor

bayadere

~

Telecommute with Teledu, X
is not enough
true tinsey
paddle boat to the
long plank, inkst
and on to inkstar

~

A scarabrecliner dripdries a
hook catenary
to aks you, Dregdrindrumlin
Y and off

U and non u to
a beepollen

drinkable predicate sunburst, o

Y.

~

So, the 31st of St Precis's day, the
scaremonger and
Meker burner, who
who and who is
she, O Melancthonian, who
the X
the X
The Y — photophobophonic — who careers to
? the.
Who.

~

YES, ladies y ladrones, at Jay it turns
back into a G;
at St Rogue's drop
U
is xspelled to
C.
C bright so.

~

TO find a gamma golden today rose in the voice as
unvoiced,
niche
nidifugous

Shied away from, shield
tempered. A glint
glimpse of the of the
of the afar owlradiopaque

my fellow X and radish

ish. sh. Fall silent now

~

A ripening West Thorn
recalculates the timbre
tam
tam
tem;

One kind of owlgrass top
is another's Trip to J.
tom
tum
tum, o;

Tin, listen to your shapely can
for it cannot mum aluminum
tum
tem
tem.

~

So, as Silvery's empty turn

drop
to
a
grave condition, actual

as the Mole's-way

delves a darkening

bloodswort

~

Deep in the Malabar nightshade, dear,
magnus hitch
is diazatized
with a swivel-type
newel. Deep in the sem-sem X

Madras, madrasah, mahoon.

~

Somewhere's wicked glove, moonpowdered,
silent, extreme.

A star goose on high,

Limbo catwalk

delivered. A dare

devilled egg.

No, no, no, no, no, no, no.

~

With a jinx upon the timing gear
an
X is lost

where St Powder frowned
in azure crystal

Dinnono. Dinoon. Din.

~

Needle growing in ancient basalt
hear
Time's
rampant chirrup. X to a turnip

is taut entablature. A no one

goad, gree.

~

A medley of whacks
watted.

Ohm's toe. Things grow cold.

~

Daylight recognitionizes

nebu
nebu
nebu
cats eat grass
under

moonish moonlight.

Things grow hot.

~

UNITED BOLT & SCREW
will
find you
out.

Down in down in down in. Out
person;
in your
featherbed of X's and O's.

Down in, down in Dumbo
where live wires

turn
the
buckle, O to off.

~

KEEP C in secret shoebox, monsoor,
for whose X
sake an unknown
oboe mmm
inaugurates an aural halo
of <u>ignes fatui</u>

~

ALL the way clear to Aliquippa

helical ticks the gear
wheel,

Kewpie Kewpie Kewpie;

radiant with nonself.

~

The Rat Minaret—

Hazarding past the
dewdrop W

you
encountercounter

a nonself

redrift as can opener.

~

Raven's woolly departure's Y top a

burnt Bernouli;

you too.

~

NO POINT MORTGAGES wilt in daynights
wild thyme;

the onus on us

a tragic lumber. Conceal your

ogive in Glitter's hole, fabulous

with real church baptism,
the crickets' reply

~

Evil Raven, have paper pity upon those
in Stamford Plaza
(plaza of streaming leaflets, land of
papers, all made of paper.)

~

Who lowers the unseen hat from on high
if not
an unseen dominion
with an unknown agenda?

~

Soon an oldy amphora
is
here & now's amphora;

grows antlered and

writin' on tables
is stupid

as the saying goes.

~

Midnight rain:

A ghost slops
from door to door

                                    asking for a real
                                        umbrella.

                    Sad, saddest Hejirah!

                                    But no one hears
                                    the fatal knock.

                              ~

Most simple things repel
each against the other.

The rule is a skid-mark of light.
Humble, yet a

frightwig's truth.

                              ~

Endowed fiction of a mouse ear,
bring to each
specific
fracture the

absolute.

Absolute ears are listening
to all things
atop the Rat Minaret.

                              ~

7 places, each a heptad nuisance because you hafta can't be too 7, see?

~

Silvery tells no sphere to go and
hawk the hat;

because the hat is oldy
she wear the fatal coat.

Silvery slips through dark reeds
like pure contrition;

like smoke.

Someone is in love with
someone no more.

~

NO tongue but bumbles, has
ne'er expressed
what the umbel
does, this caloric Fall
in perfect radiation.

~

Some one lies awake, her eye
attentive in the general sleep

as it

tosses the moon from cat to cat

a gloved cloud recalls

those long, long lashes.

~

Something saucer-eyed, O Airy, resides at
the
bottom
of thy inky porcelain.

~

CRACKED ATTICS run the gamut of ruin's
open-
faced

timber. Last puppet still

must detox debug.

O Alabama, O Alabama.

~

At the sun hub's electromagnetic
sanctorum
something
telltale
tells me I am correct to
hide all expectation.

~

Each ring tells a story in the world
before this one, too.

Three to a parable.

Four to a

treehouse, see.

~

Tell me, O silent Mahoon, which was the
turn's out;
and if a fracture in the porcelain,
which way corrected its bat
and being a dead bat,
gone and skyugled.

And they say the speaking leaf
is done.

~

What will not serve a telling
should be,
poor Witch of Agnesi,

perhaps withheld; although
a

lower, wider, deeper
fractal

Euclid be drowned
in pillow.

~

Odd raven, blow the tufted flinty char
as
you
pass over past

us: derelict and
yellow-headed, a

nonself of magpie
and other yellowyellow stuff.

~

Blue sky in a human face
the wide surprise
surprised at itself

Auntie No Hoo Hoo
has learned it all from you,

highest shelf of self:
Another something/nothing
Face of porcelain wrought

~

What has opened is a weed's
belief;

our laughter has no place
in that oubliette,

but neither has our silence.

For Celan

~

So perfectly done and yet
blank,

the show, as limned in black
velour, lost riddles and a

snatch or two upon the
singular Cuban beard.

~

If I have truly repaired the riddle
how, how how could I
not know it from the, the

fact of it
and the Airy disc
of passionate
plausibility that is
stuck there, blind rat.

~

Raven walks stick-legged to a moon
much like ours,
roundy in appearance
but of a false order of being;

only there do they repair
Raven's broken wing.

~

Moth house is taking over, Sir Footfall,
my
silvery domain.
why
scare
what's scarlet, if only
these wings

alarm me, with a mothery
of piffle, in my own

house of cards?

~

Both ways at once impossible
but double.

Both necessary to be human
a terror
and terrificity.

Light caul
in
cat's humped
fur.

A
dark call to simultaneous zig
zag
zug
swan. O

~

.00007 is not only not my lark

it is a hopeless disposal
of
a numberless

stress of mustard seed upon the

pumpkin wind, oh.

~

A slip-up master minded is a
fixture
with no plug.

A fixture with no plug,
O Airy, ought

to pass for merely human
in about a million

more seconds of anguish
over the nature
of what's

fixed and what's free

by the overturned lake.

Near Popup and Peeptown,
over second thoughts.

~

My opening is now closed again.
After 7 years
a broken glass
has told the
word
what to do:

what remains

like the shuttle cock

cannot be
shut

Down. Cannot be so simply done.

~

Up on the moon's highest pillow
Silvery
sits and shuts
her faint wing

till someone dare point the
unerring finger in her
direction.

That finger is a way of assenting
without saying "yes".

~

After is after all a fiction,
for like X
upon
Y
it is what
never arrives and and and

River runs out the tub

Bim, bam, bum.

~

Go, and find Airy her silver shoes
for
no lamp
swamp with gooey luxor
trips
and sways

deep, deep, deep in Gooner Park.

End of The Rat Minaret

Roof Books

the best in language since 1976

Selected & Recent Titles

- Dworkin, Craig. Motes. 88 p. $14.95
- Gordon, Nada. Scented Rushes. 104 p. $13.95
- Kuszai, Joel. Accidency. 120 p. $14.95.
- Tardos, Anne. Both Poems. 112 p. $14.95
- Torres, Edwin. Yes Thing No Thing. 128 p. $14.95.
- Vallejo, César. Against Professional Secrets. Translated by Joseph Mulligan. (complete Spanish/English) 104 p. $14.95.

Roof Books are published by
Segue Foundation
300 Bowery • New York, NY 10012
Visit our website at seguefoundation.com

Roof Books are distributed by
SMALL PRESS DISTRIBUTION
1341 Seventh Street • Berkeley, CA. 94710-1403.
Phone orders: 800-869-7553
spdbooks.org